My Body My Rules
A Kid's Journey Into Boundaries & Bravery
By Dr. Charmaine Marie, Ed.D.

Published by: Real LOVE Publications

My Body My Rules

A Kid's Journey Into Boundaries & Bravery

By Dr. Charmaine Marie, Ed.D.

Copyright © 2026 by: Real LOVE Publications.

All rights reserved

No part of this publication may be reproduced, stored in a retrieval system or transmitted in any way by any means, electronic, mechanical, photocopy, recording or otherwise without the prior permission of the author except as provided by USA copyright law.

This book is a work of nonfiction. Descriptions, entities, and incidents included in the story are exclusively products of the author's imagination. Any resemblance to events, and entities is entirely coincidental.

ISBN#: 978-0-578-08812-9

Printed in the United States of America

Thank you for taking the time to read,

My Body My Rules

A Kid's Journey Into Boundaries & Bravery

We hope you enjoy the book.

Please do a book review on Amazon.com

to let us know what you think.

Proverbs 25:28/Amplified Bible

**Like a city that is broken down and without walls [leaving it unprotected]
Is a man who has no self-control over his spirit [and sets himself up for trouble]**

PART 1

Intro

Chapter 1 Respect Starts With Me

Chapter 2 My Body Belongs to Me

Chapter 3 Your Hands Are Powerful

Chapter 4 The Power of NO

PART 2

Intro

Chapter 5 "NO" Is A Complete Sentence

Chapter 6 Consent: The Magic Word

Chapter 7 Trust Your Gut

Chapter 8 Safe Spaces, Safe People

Chapter 9 The Digital World

Chapter 10 Your Body, Your Rules

PART 3

Intro

Chapter 1 When a "Joke" Becomes a Crime

Chapter 2 When the Police Get Involved

Chapter 3 Courtrooms, Probation & Losing Your Freedom

Outro

PART 1

INTRO

From the moment you were born, you've had something powerful, your choices. The way you speak, the way you move, and yes, the way you use your hands. Your choices can lift people up, or tear trust down. They can protect someone's feelings, or leave a hurt that's hard to forget.

This book was created to show you the truth: you were made to protect, not to harm. You were made to respect yourself, your body, and the people around you. And every time you learn how to set boundaries and honor someone else's, you become stronger, wiser, and more prepared for the world ahead.

Sometimes, grown-ups and media send confusing messages. They joke about things that shouldn't be joked about. They make touching seem like a game. They make "being grown" look cool without telling you the consequences. But you deserve better. You deserve clarity, safety, and the confidence to make strong decisions.

So, this book will teach you:

- **How to keep your hands to yourself in every situation**
- **What respect looks like in real life**
- **How to say "no" with courage**
- **How to stop yourself from doing something that could hurt someone**
- **How to protect your own body**
- **What consent truly means**
- **And what to do if something ever feels wrong**

We're not here to scare you. We're here to prepare you. You're growing into a leader, a creator, and a protector. The world needs more people like you; people who choose respect, choose boundaries, choose kindness, and choose to do what's right even when it's not popular.

And here's the truth, great futures get ruined when kids aren't taught the right things at the right time. But you're getting the truth today, so you can grow up safe, strong, and successful, without crossing lines that break trust or break lives.

Every page of this book that you read will give you power. Power to protect yourself. Power to protect others. Power to stay on the path of greatness.

Let's begin.

CHAPTER 1

Respect Starts With Me

Respect isn't just a big word grown-ups use. Respect is a superpower that every young person can carry with them everywhere they go. It's in how you talk, how you listen, how you treat people, and how you treat yourself. Respect isn't one thing, it's the way you choose to act in every moment.

When you walk into a room, people can feel your respect before you even say a word. They feel it when you smile at them. They feel it when you speak politely. They feel it when you give someone enough space to feel comfortable. Respect is something people don't just see, they experience it.

Respect is also something that protects. When you show respect, you're telling the world:

- "I care about how you feel."

- "I care about your comfort."

- "I want to make sure you feel safe around me."

- "I value our interactions."

And when you demand respect for yourself, you're saying:

- "I deserve to be safe."
- "My body belongs to me."
- "My feelings matter."
- "I don't have to accept treatment that hurts me or makes me uncomfortable."

Respect works both ways. You give it. You expect it. You protect it. Respect + Boundaries = Safety.

Boundaries are the invisible lines that tell people how you want to be treated. They're like traffic lights we all use every day.

Green light:

- "I'm okay with that."
- "This feels good."
- "We're both comfortable."

Yellow light:

- "Slow down."
- "I'm unsure."
- "Ask before going any further."

Red light:

- "Stop."
- "I don't like this."
- "This makes me uncomfortable."

When you understand boundaries; your own and other people's, you help create a world where everyone can feel calm, safe, and respected.

Why Respect Matters So Much

Respect isn't only about being polite. It's about making sure no one feels uncomfortable, scared, embarrassed, or pressured. When you show respect, you keep people feeling safe around you. That safety helps build:

- **Stronger friendships**
- **Better communication**
- **More trust**
- **Healthier relationships**
- **A reputation people admire**

People remember how you made them feel. When respect guides your behavior, people see you as someone who can be trusted, and that is one of the greatest compliments you can receive.

Respect Protects Feelings and Bodies

Respect isn't just about words. It's also about the choices you make with your actions. Giving someone space when they look uncomfortable? That's respect. Asking before you give someone a hug? That's respect. Stopping immediately when someone says stop? That's respect. Understanding that someone's body is their own? That's BIG respect.

When you respect someone's boundaries, you protect them. When you understand your own boundaries, you protect yourself. Both matter, every single time.

Your Choices Create Your Reputation

Every day, you're creating the story people will tell about you. Not the gossip. Not the rumors. Not the chatter. But your character.

People will remember if you're gentle. People will remember if you're careful. People will remember if you listen when someone says "No." People will remember if you stop when someone is uncomfortable. And people will **DEFINITELY** remember if you don't. Respect is how you build the version of yourself you want the world to know.

TRY THIS: 3 Ways YOU Show Respect

Write down (or draw) three ways you show respect at home, at school, and with friends.

If you can't think of any right away, here are some ideas to get you started:

- "I wait my turn before speaking."

- "I don't grab people, their clothes, or their bodies."

- "I apologize if I bump into someone."

- "I ask before touching someone's things."

- "I stop immediately when someone says no or stop."

Pick three that fit YOU, because your personal respect style is part of what makes you special.

CHAPTER 2

My Body Belongs to Me

Your body is yours. Every part of it. Every inch. Every space. You were born with the right to feel safe in your own skin. Nobody; not friends, not cousins, not classmates, not teammates, not adults, not anyone, gets to decide what happens to your body except you.

This isn't a maybe. This isn't sometimes. This is an always rule. Your Body, Your Rules! Think of your body like your home. You decide who gets invited inside. You decide who stays outside. You decide what behavior is allowed and what behavior is not. Just like your home has doors, your body has boundaries. And those boundaries are not optional, they're necessary.

Some people have big boundaries: They don't like hugs, don't want people close, or prefer lots of space. Some people have smaller boundaries: They're okay with hugs from friends or playful fist bumps. Both are normal. Both are allowed. Both deserve respect.

Private Areas Stay Private

There are certain parts of your body that are called private areas. These are the parts covered by your underwear, boxers, panties, shorts, a bra, and/or a bathing suit. These areas are not for anyone else to touch, look at, talk about, or joke about. Not your friends. Not your boyfriend or girlfriend. Not a stranger. Not a family member. Not ANYONE.

And the same is true for other people, THEIR private areas are off-limits to you. We don't need scary words. We don't need grown-up explanations. We just need one rule: Nobody should ever touch your private areas, and you should never touch anyone else's.

If someone tries to, for any reason, that is a red light. A BIG one. You don't freeze. You don't hide it. You don't keep secrets. You tell a safe adult right away.

If It Feels Wrong, It Is Wrong

Your body has its own alarm system. It talks to you. Sometimes it whispers. Sometimes it yells.

Here are some signs your body gives you when something is wrong:

• **Your stomach feels tight**

• **You feel nervous or shaky**

• **You feel sick without being sick**

• **You feel confused**

• **You suddenly feel quiet or frozen**

• **You want to get away**

• **Something feels "off," even if you don't know why**

These feelings matter. Your body is trying to protect you. You don't need proof. You don't need a reason. You don't need to explain it perfectly. If your body says, "This doesn't feel right," you listen, every single time.

You Can Always Say STOP

No matter who the person is…

No matter how old they are…

No matter what they say…

No matter what they promise…

You always have the right to say:

- "Stop."
- "I don't like that."
- "Move back."
- "Don't touch me."
- "I'm uncomfortable."
- "No."

And here's the important part: You never have to feel guilty for protecting your body. Your comfort matters. Your safety matters. Your voice matters.

You're Not Responsible for Anyone Else's Behavior

Sometimes kids think:

- "Maybe I should've pushed harder."
- "Maybe I shouldn't have been there."
- "Maybe it was my fault."

No.

No.

And absolutely not.

If someone touches you in a way that's not okay, they made the wrong choice. Not you. Never you. There is nothing, NOTHING, you could do that would mean you "deserved it" or "asked for it."

Wrong is wrong, and responsibility belongs to the person who crossed the line. Tell a Safe Adult (and Keep Telling Until Someone Helps). Safe adults are people who will listen, believe you, and help you.

A safe adult could be:

- **a parent**

- **a guardian**

- **a teacher**

- **a counselor**

- **a coach**

- **a pastor**

- **a trusted family friend**

- **a school nurse**

- **your doctor**

You don't have to say everything perfectly. You don't have to use fancy words.

You can simply say:

• "Something happened, and I'm scared."

• "Someone touched me, and I didn't like it."

• "I need help."

• "I don't feel safe."

You deserve protection. You deserve support. You deserve help. And you deserve it immediately.

TRY THIS: Know Your Body's Boundaries

Write or draw your answers:

1. List three people you feel safe talking to.

2. Write one sentence that reminds you: "My body belongs to me."

3. Circle a color that feels like safety: red, yellow, green, blue, or purple.

4. Why does that color make you feel safe?

CHAPTER 3

Your Hands Are Powerful

Your hands are powerful. They can build, create, help, and protect. They can lift someone up, make someone smile, and show kindness without saying a single word. Your hands can make the world better, or they can cause harm. And every day, you get to choose how you use them.

Think of your hands as tools. Tools can fix things, or they can break things. Tools aren't bad, and they aren't good, it all depends on how the person holding them decides to use them.

Hands Are Meant for Helping, Not Hurting

Your hands should never be used to scare someone, surprise someone in a way that makes them uncomfortable, or touch someone's body without permission. Even if you think it's a joke, even if you're "just playing," even if you didn't mean anything by it, touching someone without their agreement is always a problem.

Helpful hands:
- Lift someone up when they fall
- Hold your books
- Create art
- Write your dreams
- Give a high-five
- Clap for someone
- Help carry groceries
- Wash dishes
- Build something amazing
- Pet a dog or cat
- Help a younger kid learn something new

Harmful hands:

- Grabbing someone
- Touching someone's body without permission
- Hitting, pinching, poking, slapping
- "Joking" touches that make someone uncomfortable
- Touching private areas
- Pressuring someone to do something
- Blocking someone's path so they can't move
- Pulling on someone's clothes or body

Your hands tell a story about who you are. Make sure that story is one you're proud of.

"I'm Just Playing" Doesn't Make It Okay

Sometimes people use their hands in ways that make others uncomfortable and then try to cover it up by saying:

- "I was just joking!"
- "Relax!"
- "I didn't mean anything!"
- "It's not that serious!"
- "It was just a game!"

But here's the truth: If someone feels uncomfortable, confused, unsafe, or disrespected, that matters more than any joke.

Play should be fun for everyone. If only one person is having fun, and the other person feels scared or uncomfortable, then it's not play. It's pressure.

Hands should never be used to trick, embarrass, or confuse someone. That's not a joke, it's disrespect.

Ask First. Always. Before touching someone, even for things that seem small, always ask:

- "Can I hug you?"

- "Is it okay if I sit here?"

- "Do you want to play?"

- "Can I touch your hair?"

- "Do you want a high-five?"

If the answer is no, your hands stay with you. Asking before you act shows that you respect the other person's body and feelings. It also shows that you understand one of the most important life skills you will ever learn: consent.

If Someone Pulls Away, That's a No

Sometimes people don't say "no" with their words, they say it with their body:

- They step back
- They move sideways
- They turn away
- They freeze
- They look uncomfortable
- They don't smile
- They don't laugh
- Their body stiffens

These are all signs that they are not comfortable. When you see these signs, it's not your job to argue or guess, it's your job to stop immediately.

Your Hands Show Your Heart

What you do with your hands tells people something about you.

Hands that respect others say:

"I care."

"I listen."

"I want you to feel safe around me."

"I know how to make good choices."

"I understand boundaries."

Hands that don't respect boundaries say the opposite. Every day, you get to choose who you want to be, the protector or the pressure-maker. And being a protector is always the right choice.

You're Responsible for Your Actions

Even if you didn't mean to make someone uncomfortable, even if you didn't think it was a big deal, even if you didn't know better, once you learn the right way, it becomes your responsibility to do better.

Growing up means understanding that your actions have consequences. And using your hands in the wrong way can seriously hurt someone's feelings, body, confidence, and/or safety. You are responsible for the way you choose to use your hands, every second, every minute, every day.

TRY THIS: 10 Good Things Your Hands Can Do

Grab a blank piece of paper and write or draw 10 positive things your hands can do.

Here are some ideas to help:

- Make art
- Hold someone's hand if they're scared
- Take notes in class
- Write poetry or music
- Plant something
- Help clean
- Learn a new skill
- Bake or cook
- Wave at someone
- Build something creative

Circle your top three favorites.

These are your hand superpowers, use them often.

CHAPTER 4

The Power of NO

No is one of the strongest safety tools you will ever have. It's a small word with big power, a word that protects your body, your feelings, your comfort, and your space. Saying "no" is not rude. It's not disrespectful. It's not selfish. It's not dramatic.

Saying "no" is smart.

Saying "no" is safe.

Saying "no" is your right.

When you say "no," you're not trying to hurt someone's feelings. You're trying to protect yourself, and that is something you should never apologize for.

No Is a Full Sentence

You don't have to explain why you don't want something. You don't have to give excuses. You don't have to argue your point. You don't have to make it sound nice.

Sometimes the strongest and safest thing you can do is use your voice clearly and confidently:

"No."

"I don't want to."

"Stop."

"Don't touch me."

"I'm not comfortable."

"That's not okay with me."

Be Clear. Be Direct. Be Strong. That is the language of boundaries.

You Don't Owe Anyone Access to Your Body

You don't have to hug people if you don't want to. You don't have to sit close to someone if it makes you uncomfortable. You don't have to let anyone touch you; not your hands, not your shoulders, not your hair, not your clothes, and definitely not your private areas.

No one gets access to your body just because they're older than you, because they're related to you, because they're your friend, because they always do this, or because they say, you're overreacting. Your boundaries are yours, and nobody else's opinion changes them!

You Can Say No at Any Time

You can say no at the beginning. You can say no in the middle. You can say no at the end. You can say no even if you said yes earlier.

Changed your mind?

Not comfortable anymore?

Feeling pressure?

Something feels wrong?

Say no, and everything should stop. That is what consent means: If you're not comfortable, the answer is no, always.

No Protects Your Space

Imagine your personal space as a bubble around your body. Inside that bubble is peace, comfort, and safety. Everyone has a bubble: you, your friends, your classmates, and your family.

You get to decide who enters your bubble. You get to decide who stays out. You get to decide how close someone can get. And if someone steps into your bubble without permission? You have the right to push that bubble back out with your words:

- "Back up."

- "Move away."
- "Please give me space."

These boundaries protect your bubble and your peace.

You're Not "Mean" for Saying No

Some people try to make you feel guilty for using your boundaries:

- "I was just playing!"
- "Wow, you're being dramatic."
- "I didn't mean it like that."
- "You're no fun."
- "Relax."

Do Not Ignore it! Here's the truth: People who respect you will respect your no. People who don't, aren't people you need in your space.

Saying "no" does not make you mean. Pressuring someone after they say no? That's what's mean.

Different Ways to Say No

Sometimes "no" needs to be strong. Sometimes it needs to be firm. Sometimes you can say it with your body language.

Here are a few options:

Be Calm and Clear:

"No, I don't like that."

"I don't want to do that."

Be Strong and Serious:

"Stop now."

"Get off me."

"That's not okay."

Body Language No:

Pulling away

Stepping back

Turning around

Shielding your body

Not engaging

Your body can say no even if your voice is quiet, and that still counts.

It's Courageous to Protect Yourself

It takes strength to use your voice. It takes confidence to set boundaries. It takes bravery to say no and mean it.

Every time you say no to something that feels unsafe, uncomfortable, or pressured, you are choosing safety over silence, and that is powerful. You are teaching people how they must treat you. You are setting the rules. You are protecting your future. And that makes you strong.

TRY THIS: Practice 5 NO Statements

Write or practice these out loud:

1. "No, stop that!"

2. "I don't want you touching me!"

3. "Move away from me!"

4. "I'm not comfortable! Stop!"

5. "No! That's my boundary!"

Say them until they feel natural. Say them until you believe them. Say them until using your voice becomes second nature. Your voice is your protection, use it boldly.

PART 2

INTRO

Practice Makes Protection

So far, this book has been speaking directly to you, teaching you about your body, your boundaries, your power, and your right to say no. You've learned important truths about respect, consent, and keeping your hands to yourself. Now it's time for something a little different.

This part of the book is not just for you. It is for you and a trusted adult, such as a parent, caregiver, or guardian, to explore together. Why? Because knowing the rules is only the beginning. Real life doesn't always come with clear instructions.

Sometimes situations feel confusing. Sometimes people joke when they shouldn't. Sometimes pressure shows up quietly. Sometimes you don't know what to say until it's already happening.

That's where this section comes in. In Part Two, you will read real-life scenarios and teaching moments that show:

- What situations might look like
- Why certain choices lead to problems
- What to say when something feels wrong

- What to do to protect yourself and others
- How to make smart, respectful decisions, even when it's hard

These chapters are designed to help you practice, not to scare you, blame you, or shame you. You'll also notice something important:

- This section talks more with you

It opens the door for conversation, questions, and honest discussions with the adults who care about you. There are no bad questions here, only learning moments.

Mistakes don't have to turn into harm. Confusion doesn't have to turn into consequences. And situations don't have to spiral when you know what to say and do.

This is where knowledge turns into action, learning becomes protection, and where respect shows up in real life. Let's walk through it together.

CHAPTER 5

No Is A Complete Sentence

Teaching Kids the Power, Purpose, and Protection of the Word That Saves Lives

If you ask most adults what the hardest word is for young people to say, they'll tell you it's no. Not because kids don't understand it; kids say no to chores, vegetables, and bedtime like pros! But when it comes to protecting themselves, standing up for their boundaries, or stopping someone from pushing them into something uncomfortable, suddenly that little two-letter word feels heavy.

This chapter is designed to take the fear, guilt, and awkwardness out of saying no, and replace it with confidence, courage, and clarity. Because when young people understand that no is their right, their shield, and their voice, they become safer, stronger, and harder to manipulate.

We're teaching the kind of NO that echoes. The kind that stands tall even if a person or situation tries to bend it. The kind that saves futures.

Let's break it down.

Section 1: Understanding Why No Is So Powerful

No is a boundary. It's not rude. It's not mean. It's not disrespectful. It's protection.

When a young person says no, they are:

• Guarding their body

• Defending their safety

• Taking control of their choices

• Making sure their voice is respected

• Preventing anyone from touching or pressuring them

Section 2: Why Some Kids Struggle to Say No

Kids hesitate because:

- **They don't want to hurt anyone's feelings**
- **They don't want to get in trouble**
- **They feel embarrassed**
- **Someone older told them they have to**
- **They were raised to be polite even when uncomfortable**
- **They think adults or friends know best**
- **They don't want to seem uncool or difficult**
- **They worry no one will believe them**

We have to teach them: Your safety is more important than someone's feelings, every single time.

Section 3: No Means No, Every Time and for Everyone

This is the rule: If a child says no, the conversation stops. The touching stops. The pressure stops. The moment stops.

No exceptions.

No "but I thought…"

No "but we're just playing…"

No "but we're friends…"

No "but I'm older…"

No "but you didn't say anything before…"

When no shows up, everything else sits down.

Section 4: How to Say No With Strength (Even When You're Nervous)

Not every no has to be loud. But every no must be clear.

Different ways youth can say no:

Direct No: "No, stop."

Firm No: "I don't want to do that. Back up."

Body Language No: Stepping back, turning away, moving out of reach.

Exit No: Walking away and going to a safe person.

Voice + Exit No: "No. I'm leaving."

Help-Seeking No: "No. I'm getting an adult."

Public No: "No! Stop touching me."

Whatever approach they use, the mission is the same: protect yourself first.

Section 5: Respecting Other People's No

This chapter isn't just about helping kids say no. It's also about preventing future harm by teaching kids to honor someone else's no, without debate, persuasion, attitude, or frustration. We're shaping a world of youth who don't grow into adults who pressure or violate others.

Teach them:

- If someone says no, you stop immediately.

- If someone moves away, you stop immediately.

- If someone seems uncomfortable, you stop immediately.

- If someone doesn't answer, that's a no too.

No is not the beginning of negotiation. It is the end of the conversation.

Section 6: Real-Life Scenarios (With "What to Do" Tips)

Scenario 1: A Friend Wants a Hug

Friend: "Come on, just give me a hug."

You: "No thanks, I don't feel like it."

Tip: You never owe physical affection. Not even to friends.

Scenario 2: Someone Teasingly Touches Your Hair or Clothes

You: "Don't touch me like that."

Tip: Jokes stop being jokes the moment you feel uncomfortable.

Scenario 3: Someone Older Says, "Don't Tell Anyone, It's Our Secret"

You: "No. I'm telling."

Tip: Safe adults NEVER ask kids for private secrets involving touching or bodies.

Scenario 4: A Teen Tries to Pressure You Into a Kiss

You: "No. I'm not doing that. Move back."

Tip: Consent is required every single time.

Scenario 5: You Feel Frozen

Sometimes kids freeze up.

If that happens:

- Move away
- Go toward a public area
- Call out
- Find a safe adult

Even if your voice feels stuck, your feet can still say no.

Section 7: Activity - Finding Your No Voice

Activity: Have students write down three ways they can say "no" in their own style (polite, funny, bold, calm, direct).

Examples:

- "Nah, I'm good."
- "No for me, thanks."
- "Nope. That's not okay."
- "Stop right there."
- "Back up. Now."

This teaches them to use their natural tone, so their no feels comfortable and real.

Section 8: Reflection Questions

1. What makes it hard for you to say no?

2. Who are three adults you feel safe saying no around?

3. What does your body feel like when something doesn't feel right?

4. How do you want others to treat your boundaries?

5. How will you practice using your no this week?

Section 9: Key Takeaways

• No protects your body and your boundaries.

• You never owe anyone access to your space.

• You don't need a reason to say no.

• Your no is enough, even if others don't like it.

• Saying no builds confidence and stops unsafe situations.

• Respecting other people's no is just as important as having your own.

Your no is your power.

Your no is your voice.

Your no is your right.

And the youth who learn to use their NO become adults who respect it, in themselves and others.

CHAPTER 6

Consent: The Magic Word

Teaching Young People That Nothing Moves Forward Without a Real, Honest, Confident Yes

Consent is one of the most important skills a young person can learn, not just for safety, but for relationships, friendships, and life as a whole. It's the difference between respect and harm, comfort and discomfort, and safety and danger.

Consent is not a grown-up word. It's a life word, and youth deserve to understand it early, plainly, and powerfully.

Today we teach them the truth: Nothing involving someone's body, space, or feelings is allowed unless every person involved says a clear, happy, pressure-free YES.

Anything else is a no. Anything uncertain is a no. Anything silent is a no. Anything forced is a no. Anything rushed is a no. Let's break down consent until it becomes second nature.

Section 1: What Consent Really Means

Consent is:

- **A clear agreement**
- **Made freely**
- **With no pressure**
- **No fear**
- **No guilt**
- **No tricks**
- **No confusion**
- **No guessing**
- **No manipulation**
- **No embarrassment**
- **No just go along with it**

Consent is someone saying: "I want this. I feel good about this. I choose this." If that's not what's happening, then consent is not happening.

Section 2: Consent Is Required Every Time

A yes from last week doesn't count today. A yes from a previous situation doesn't count for a new one. A yes to something small doesn't equal a yes to something bigger. Consent is moment-by-moment. Just like you have to ask before borrowing a person's belongings, you have to ask before entering their space.

The rule: If you didn't check, you don't have consent. If you assumed, you don't have consent. If you pressured, you definitely don't have consent.

Section 3: Consent Is More Than Words

People show their feelings through:

- **Body language**
- **Facial expressions**
- **Comfort level**
- **Movement**
- **Energy**
- **Tone**
- **Silence**

Teach youth to pay attention. If someone:

- **Pulls back**
- **Looks uncomfortable**
- **Avoids eye contact**
- **Stays quiet**
- **Laughs nervously**
- **Freezes**
- **Doesn't join in**
- **Seems unsure**

That is NOT consent. That is a red light. And red means STOP, not "keep trying."

Section 4: How to Ask for Consent

Youth need simple and safe language they can use without awkwardness or fear. Here are healthy ways to check in:

• "Is this okay?"

• "Do you want to?"

• "Are you comfortable right now?"

• "I want to make sure you're good with this."

• "If you want to stop, just say so."

• "It's okay to say no."

Be Short. Be Clear. Be Respectful. Be Confident. A person who respects boundaries never fears asking.

Section 5: Consent Requires a Happy, Pressure-Free Yes

A real yes sounds like:

- "Yes, that's fine."
- "Yes, I'm okay with that."
- "Yes, let's do it."
- "Yes, I feel safe."

Not just words, but a comfortable vibe.

If the answer is:

- "Uhhh…"
- "Maybe…"
- "I guess…"
- "I don't know…"
- Shoulder shrug
- Nervous laughter

That's a no, not a "sort of."

Teach youth:

A real yes feels good.

A pressured yes is still a no.

Section 6: When Consent Is Impossible

Consent cannot exist if someone is:

• **Too young**

• **Scared**

• **Threatened**

• **Manipulated**

• **Bribed**

• **Tricked**

• **Sleepy**

• **Unaware**

• **Confused**

• **Drunk or high (for teens & adults)**

• **Afraid of consequences**

If someone cannot think clearly or choose freely, they cannot consent. Period. No exceptions. No excuses. We're not raising future offenders. We're raising future protectors.

Section 7: Respecting the Right to Change Their Mind

A huge part of teaching consent is helping youth understand: Anyone can change their mind at any time. And as soon as they do, everything stops. Teach them this script: "It's okay if you're not comfortable anymore. Thank you for telling me."

No anger.

No guilt trips.

No attitude.

Respect is the response.

Section 8: Real-Life Scenarios (And What Consent Looks Like)

Scenario 1: A Friend Wants a Piggyback Ride

Friend: "Give me a piggyback ride!"

You: "Are you sure you want one?"

Friend: "Yes!"

Green light.

Scenario 2: Someone Puts Their Arm Around You Without Asking, and You Move Away.

Them: "What's wrong?"

You: "I don't like being touched like that."

Them: "Okay, I won't do that again."

Respect.

Scenario 3: A Teen Asks You to Kiss Them

You: "I'm not comfortable with that."

Them: "Okay, cool. I respect that."

That's what healthy looks like.

Scenario 4: A Person Does Not Speak Up At All

Silence = No.

Silence is NEVER consent.

Scenario 5: A Friend Says Yes, but Looks Nervous

Words say yes.

Body says no.

Stop.

Check in.

Respect their comfort, not just their answer.

Section 9: Activity The "Green, Yellow, Red Light Game"

This exercise helps youth understand boundaries quickly.

Green Light (Yes):

- **Comfortable**
- **Relaxed**
- **Smiling**
- **Saying yes clearly**

Yellow Light (Unsure):

- **Hesitant**
- **Quiet**
- **Not fully okay**
- **Mixed feelings**
- **Shrugging**
- **"I guess"**

Red Light (Stop):

- **Saying no**
- **Pulling away**
- **Looking upset or scared**
- **Frozen**
- **Avoiding**
- **Crying**
- **Silent**

Section 10: Reflection Questions

1. What does real consent mean to you?

2. How can you tell when someone is uncomfortable?

3. Why is it important to ask before entering someone's space?

4. How does it feel to know you have the right to say yes and no?

5. How will you show respect for other people's boundaries?

Section 11: Key Takeaways

- **Consent keeps people safe.**
- **Consent must be voluntary, clear, and happy.**
- **Silence is a no.**
- **Uncertainty is a no.**
- **Pressure makes everything a no.**
- **You can change your mind at any time.**
- **Respect is non-negotiable.**
- **If you don't have consent, you don't have permission.**

Consent is respect. Consent is safety. Consent is kindness. Consent is maturity. Consent is protection. And when youth learn it early, they grow into adults who protect, not harm.

CHAPTER 7

Trust Your Gut

Helping Young People Recognize Red Flags, Listen to Their Inner Warning System, and Stay Safe

Every human being; kids, teens, and adults, comes with a built-in alarm system. Some people call it instinct. Some say it's intuition. Some say it's discernment. Kids usually call it a weird feeling or say something felt off. Whatever you call it, it is your inner protector, and when it speaks, you should listen.

This chapter teaches youth how to recognize danger signals, avoid risky situations, and trust themselves even when someone else tries to downplay their feelings. Because their body knows the truth long before their brain finds the words. This chapter empowers them to stop, notice, and act.

Section 1: Your Gut Feeling Is Your First Safety Superpower

Everyone has felt it:

• The sudden nervous feeling around a certain person

• The uncomfortable vibe when someone stands too close

• That tight feeling in your chest when a situation doesn't feel safe

• That stomach drop when someone asks you to keep a secret

• That moment when something feels off, even if you can't explain it

That feeling is not random. It's not dramatic. It's not silly. It's not you overreacting. It's your body whispering, pay attention, and listening to your body can keep you safe.

Section 2: Why Kids Sometimes Ignore Their Gut

Young people often ignore their instincts because:

• They don't want to be rude

• They think adults always know best

• They feel pressured to "go along"

• They don't trust themselves yet

• They don't want to get someone in trouble

• They think they're imagining it

• They don't want conflict

• Someone told them to stop being dramatic

But here's the truth: Your safety matters more than someone's feelings. Your comfort matters more than someone's opinion. Your body belongs to you, not to anyone else.

Section 3: Red Flag Behaviors Youth Should Watch For

Young people need concrete examples.

Here are danger signs:

Red Flag #1: Someone gives you uncomfortable attention: Too many compliments, too many comments about your body, and too much interest in your personal life.

Red Flag #2: Someone tries to isolate you by saying: Come talk to me privately. Let's keep this between us. You don't have to tell your parents. Safety grows in the open, not in secrets.

Red Flag #3: Someone doesn't respect your space: Standing too close, touching without permission, and ignoring your discomfort.

Red Flag #4: Someone uses authority to control you by saying: I'm older, so listen to me. You have to do what I say. No one will believe you. Big red flag. Huge.

Red Flag #5: Someone gives gifts or favors with strings attached: If I buy you this, you owe me. After all I've done for you. Safe people give freely, not to control.

Red Flag #6: Someone pressures you to do something you don't want to do by saying: Just try it. Don't be lame. You're making a big deal out of nothing. No is no. No matter what.

Section 4: What Feeling Unsafe Looks Like Inside Your Body

Youth don't always recognize danger mentally, but their body always knows.

Signs include:

• **Stomach tightening**

• **Feeling frozen**

• **Sweaty palms**

• **Fast heartbeat**

• **Wanting to run or hide**

• **Feeling dizzy**

• **Feeling heavy or trapped**

• **A sudden mood shift**

• **Feeling like you want to cry**

If any of these show up, your body is sending a message: Get away. Tell someone. Act now.

Section 5: How to Respond When Something Feels Wrong

Teach youth the three-step safety plan:

1. Leave immediately! You don't need permission. You don't need a reason. You don't need an explanation. Just walk away.

2. Go to a safe person; A trusted adult such as:

- **Parent**
- **Guardian**
- **Counselor**
- **Teacher**
- **Coach**
- **Pastor**
- **Family friend**
- **School staff**

Someone who listens, protects, and believes you.

3. Tell the truth about what you felt, even if you don't have all the details, even if you feel embarrassed, and even if you're not sure why it felt wrong. Let them help you sort it out.

Section 6: It's Okay to Make a Scene

Kids often hesitate because they worry about:

• **Causing drama**

• **Embarrassing someone**

• **Being extra**

• **Looking rude**

• **Being judged**

Let's make something clear: If your safety feels threatened, GO FULL BROADWAY. Shout. Run. Get loud. Get help. Embarrassment fades, safety doesn't. Your safety is more important than someone's comfort.

Section 7: Real-Life Scenarios (And What to Do)

Scenario 1: An older teen keeps trying to be alone with you

Your gut says: This feels wrong.

Action: Leave the room. Tell a trusted adult.

Scenario 3: A friend dares you to do something sexual as a joke

Your stomach twists.

Action: Say no. Walk off. Don't entertain nonsense. Tell a trusted adult.

Scenario 4: A family friend tries to hug or touch you too often. Your body feels tight.

Action: Step back. Say no. Move toward others. Tell a trusted adult.

Scenario 5: Someone says, Don't tell anyone we talked about this. Your mind says, That's weird.

Action: Tell a trusted adult, immediately.

Section 8: Activity "Listen to Your Body Map"

Have youth draw a simple outline of a body (or use a printed one).

Then instruct them to:

• Mark where they feel discomfort when something doesn't feel right

• Mark where they feel safe or relaxed

• Share examples of moments when their body warned them

This helps them trust physical signals.

Section 9: Reflection Questions

1. When was a time your body warned you about something?

2. What does your gut feeling feel like?

3. Why is it important to listen to your instincts?

4. Who can you go to when something feels wrong?

5. How can you support a friend who felt unsafe?

Section 10: Key Takeaways

- **Your instincts are a gift.**
- **If something feels wrong, it probably is.**
- **You don't need evidence to walk away.**
- **You owe nobody access to your body.**
- **Creepy behavior doesn't get a second chance.**
- **Safety comes first, always.**
- **You can ALWAYS tell a safe adult.**

Your gut feeling is not your enemy, it's your protector. It speaks softly but powerfully. And when youth learn to trust it, you step into confidence, clarity, and safety.

CHAPTER 8

Safe Spaces, Safe People

Teaching Youth How to Identify Real Support, Avoid Dangerous People, and Build Their Circle of Protection

One of the most powerful lessons a young person can learn is this - You are never alone: even when something scary happens, even when someone tries to intimidate you, and even when you feel confused or embarrassed.

There are safe people in the world whose entire purpose is to protect, listen, and help. But youth can't use their support system if they don't know how to recognize who is truly safe.

This chapter helps them understand:

• Who they can trust

• How to know someone is unsafe

• Where to go if they need help

• How to speak up without fear

• Why reporting is not snitching, it's saving themselves or someone else. Let's guide them toward safety, confidence, and clarity.

Section 1: What Is a Safe Person?

A safe person is someone who:

- **Believes you**
- **Does not blame you**
- **Protects your privacy**
- **Helps you get out of danger**
- **Listens without judgment**
- **Encourages you to speak up**
- **Does not get upset when you set boundaries**
- **Never asks you to keep secrets about bodies or touching**
- **Respects your no**
- **Makes you feel seen, heard, and secure**

A safe person's presence feels like a warm blanket, not a cold warning.

Section 2: How to Recognize a Safe Person (Especially for Youth)

A safe person will:

- Ask permission before touching you - "Is it okay if I hug you?"
- Respect your boundaries - No doesn't hurt their feelings, they honor it.
- Help you feel calmer, not more confused
- Never pressure you - Not for affection. Not for attention. Not for silence. Not for secrets.
- Tell you the truth - Even if it's tough. Even if it's uncomfortable. Honesty is protection.
- Support you when you speak up - They don't dismiss or minimize your experience. Safe adults protect. Safe friends respect. Safe people never need secrets.

Section 3: What Is an Unsafe Person?

An unsafe person is anyone who:

• **Ignores your boundaries**

• **Makes you uncomfortable**

• **Wants private conversations about bodies or touching**

• **Asks you to keep secrets**

• **Makes you feel guilty for saying no**

• **Says things like Don't tell your parents**

• **Tries to control or isolate you**

• **Uses fear or intimidation**

• **Blames you for their behavior**

• **Gets angry when you speak up**

• **Pressures you in any way**

Unsafe people don't always look dangerous. Sometimes they smile. Sometimes they help with homework. Sometimes they give gifts. That's why we teach youth to trust behavior, not appearances.

Section 4: How to Build a Personal Safety Circle

Every young person should choose 3–5 safe adults they can go to anytime. Help them create what we call a Safety Circle, their personal team of protectors.

Examples:

- Parent or guardian
- Teacher or counselor
- Family member
- Church leader
- School staff member
- Coach
- Mentor
- Trusted neighbor

These should be people they feel comfortable with, and people who respect their boundaries.

Teach youth:

If one person doesn't listen, tell another, and another, and another; until someone helps. There is no limit to how many times you can speak up.

Section 5: How to Ask for Help Without Fear

Young people often hesitate because:

- They feel embarrassed
- They worry adults won't believe them
- They fear getting someone in trouble
- They think it was their fault
- They don't want to make things worse

Teach them these truths:

- You will not get in trouble for telling the truth
- You are not responsible for someone else's bad behavior
- Safe adults will always want to protect you
- You deserve help, no matter what
- Speaking up is a strength, not betrayal

Make it normal for them to talk about feelings, instincts, and unsafe situations.

Section 6: What To Say When You Need Help

Give youth simple scripts to use when they feel scared or unsure.

Short & Straightforward:

"I'm uncomfortable."

"Something happened, and I need to talk to you."

"I don't feel safe."

"I need help."

Clear & Honest:

"That person touched me, and I didn't like it."

"I think someone is being inappropriate with me."

"I don't want to be alone with them."

"This felt wrong and I need to tell someone."

Urgent:

"Come now."

"I need you. Right now."

"I am scared."

These phrases require courage and honesty.

Section 7: Where to Go if You Can't Find a Safe Person Nearby

If the situation is immediate or dangerous:

• Move into a public space

• Go where other adults are

• Head to a teacher, office, cashier, or front desk

• Call 911 if you are in real danger

• Use your phone to contact a trusted adult

• Tell any adult until one takes action

Youth need to know: You do not have to solve a dangerous situation alone.

Section 8: Telling Is Not Snitching, It's Saving

A lot of young people hesitate because of the no snitching culture.

Let's clarify: Snitching is when someone tells to get someone in trouble for something small, like a tattletale.

Telling is when someone speaks up to:

• Protect themselves

• Protect someone else

• Stop inappropriate behavior

• Prevent future harm

• Keep their body and mind safe

Speaking up about abuse, danger, manipulation, or inappropriate touching is not snitching. It's survival. It's courage. It's wisdom.

Section 9: Real-Life Scenarios (What to Do)

Scenario 1: A family friend gives you uncomfortable hugs - Tell a parent, mentor, or teacher.

Scenario 2: A classmate touches you as a joke - Move away, say stop, and tell an adult.

Scenario 3: Someone asks you to keep a secret about touching - Tell immediately, NO QUESTIONS ASKED.

Scenario 4: A teen tries to pressure you when no one is around - Leave at once. Tell your safety circle.

Scenario 5: You feel weird around someone but don't know why - Tell anyway. Feelings don't lie.

Section 10: Activity - My Safety Circle List

Have youth write down the names of their 3–5 safe adults.

Then ask them to answer:

• Why do I trust this person?

• How can I reach them?

• How can they help me when I feel unsafe?

This teaches them who to go to before anything ever happens.

Section 11: Reflection Questions

1. Who do you trust when something feels wrong?

2. How do you know someone is a safe person?

3. What makes someone unsafe?

4. How would you ask for help if you needed it today?

5. Why is it important to tell, even if you feel scared?

Section 12: Key Takeaways

• **Safe people protect, listen, and believe you.**

• **Unsafe people cross boundaries, pressure, or manipulate.**

• **Your voice matters.**

• **You are never alone.**

• **Asking for help is a strength.**

• **Your safety circle will always support you.**

• **Telling saves lives; yours and others.**

You deserve to feel safe, respected, and protected. You deserve adults who take you seriously. You deserve friends who honor your boundaries, and you deserve a world where your voice keeps you safe.

Your safety circle is your team. Lean on them. Use them. Trust them. They are here for you.

CHAPTER 9

The Digital World

Helping Youth Protect Themselves from Cyber Predators, Sexting Pressure, and Unsafe Digital Interactions

We live in a world where our phones, tablets, and computers are part of everyday life. Social media, messaging apps, and games are fun ways to connect with friends, but they also create opportunities for unsafe behavior.

Just like we teach youth to protect their bodies in the real world, we must teach them to protect themselves online. The rules don't change: boundaries, consent, and safety are still key. This chapter gives youth the tools they need to navigate the digital world confidently and safely.

Section 1: Online Safety Is Real Safety

Some youth think: It's online, it's not real, so it's safe. Wrong.

Predators can use:

- **Chat rooms**
- **Gaming apps**
- **Social media**
- **Direct messages**
- **Fake profiles**
- **Photos, videos, and posts**

…to manipulate, pressure, or trick young people. If something feels wrong online, it is wrong, just like in real life.

Section 2: The Rules for Protecting Yourself Online

1. **Never share personal information**: Full name, address, school, phone number, birthday, or location should be private.

2. **Never share photos that make you uncomfortable**: If it feels too revealing, risky, or unsafe, don't send it.

3. **Trust your gut**: If someone online makes you feel weird, pressured, or unsafe, stop talking immediately.

4. **Block and report**: Social media apps have safety features. Use them. Don't hesitate.

5. **Tell a safe adult**: If someone asks you to do something inappropriate online, tell your parent, guardian, or mentor immediately.

6. **Remember: online friends are not automatically safe**: Some may pretend to be your age or to have your best interests at heart, but are predators in disguise.

Section 3: Sexting and Digital Boundaries

Sexting = sending sexual messages, pictures, or videos. Youth must know:

- Once it's sent, it's out of your control
- It can be shared, forwarded, or used to manipulate
- Pressure from anyone to send explicit content is wrong and illegal in many places
- Saying no to sexting is always your right

Red flags online:

- "Don't tell anyone"
- "Just for me"
- "I'll be upset if you don't"
- Threats or guilt to get you to send content

Your body and privacy are never for sale, online or offline.

Section 4: Recognizing Cyber Predators

Predators often:

- Pretend to be your age
- Give lots of attention or gifts
- Try to isolate you from friends or family
- Ask for pictures or secrets
- Say they love you very quickly
- Guilt you into meeting in person
- Try to convince you that your parents won't understand

Teach youth: If someone online makes you uncomfortable, it's not your fault. Stop talking and tell an adult.

Section 5: How to Respond Safely Online

Step 1: Stop all communication. Block the person immediately.

Step 2: Save evidence: Screenshots, messages, and emails, keep them for trusted adults.

Step 3: Tell a safe adult: Parent, teacher, counselor, mentor; anyone you trust.

Step 4: Do not meet in person. Never agree to meet someone from online without a trusted adult.

Step 5: Protect your digital footprint. Once online, your content can last forever. Only share what you are comfortable with everyone seeing.

Section 6: Peer Pressure Online

Teens may pressure each other to:

- Share photos or videos
- Join private groups
- Spread gossip
- Participate in risky online challenges

Teach youth to:

- Say no confidently
- Walk away from pressure
- Remember they are not "uncool" for protecting themselves
- Recognize that respecting their boundaries online is the same as in real life

Section 7: Activity - "Digital Safety Checklist"

Have youth create a personal checklist for online safety. Examples:

- Never share personal info
- Only accept friend requests from people I know
- Always tell a trusted adult if I feel uncomfortable
- Block and report inappropriate behavior
- Never meet someone from online alone
- Think before I post or send anything

Youth can post it near their desk or save it on their device as a daily reminder.

Section 8: Reflection Questions

1. How do you know if someone online is safe?

2. What would you do if someone asked for a photo or a secret?

3. Why is it important to protect personal information online?

4. Who can you talk to if something online makes you uncomfortable?

5. How can you help friends stay safe online too?

Section 9: Key Takeaways

• Your safety online is just as important as in the real world.

• Respect your boundaries and say no to pressure.

• Predators can be anyone, even someone who seems nice or your age.

• Block, report, and tell a safe adult.

• Once content is online, it may never be fully gone.

• Protect your digital footprint like you protect your body.

• Helping friends stay safe online is part of looking out for each other.

The internet is a tool; it can be fun, educational, and social. But it can also be dangerous. Teaching young people to protect themselves online, recognize predators, and set digital boundaries keeps them safe, confident, and empowered.

Your screen doesn't replace your instincts. Your gut matters online, too. Stay alert, stay smart, and always reach out to safe adults when in doubt.

CHAPTER 10

Your Body, Your Rules

Teaching Youth Self-Respect, Boundaries, and Confidence for a Lifetime

If you've made it this far, congratulations! You now know:

- Boundaries are your best friend
- Consent is not optional
- Your gut feeling is powerful
- Safe people exist
- Online safety is real safety

But now, it's time for the most important lesson, Your body, your rules. Every youth deserves to feel confident, protected, and in charge of their own body, no exceptions. This chapter helps young people take full control, feel empowered, and make choices that protect them now and in the future.

Section 1: Respect Yourself First

Self-respect is the foundation of safety.

Youth must know:

• Saying no is brave, not rude

• Protecting your body is your right

• You deserve to be treated with kindness, respect, and dignity

• You don't need to explain your no

• Confidence in your boundaries inspires others to respect you

Self-respect is like a shield; once it's up, it helps keep danger out.

Section 2: Boundaries Are Your Superpower

Boundaries are rules about:

• Who can touch you

• Who can speak to you in certain ways

• Who can see your body or personal information

• Who you spend time with

• How close people can get to you

Boundaries are never negotiable. A person who truly respects you will never try to cross them.

Youth should practice:

• "Stop. I don't want that."

• "I don't like that. Please move back."

• "No. That's my body."

• "I'm not comfortable sharing that."

Section 3: Confidence Comes From Saying No

Saying no isn't just about rejecting someone else, it's about affirming yourself.

Teach youth:

- **No is clear, strong, and enough**
- **No protects your body, mind, and future**
- **No sets the tone for respect**
- **No gives power back to you**

Confidence grows when youth know they can say no without guilt, fear, or apology.

Section 4: How to Stand Up Without Feeling Scared

It's normal to feel nervous when asserting yourself, especially with peers or adults.

Teach youth:

1. Stand tall, don't slouch
2. Make eye contact if safe
3. Speak clearly, calmly, and firmly
4. Use simple statements:
- "I don't want that."
- "Please stop."
- "I said no."
5. Remove yourself from unsafe situations if possible
6. Go to a safe adult immediately. Even if your words feel small, your courage is huge.

Section 5: Positive Peer Influence

Youth often follow friends. Teach them:

- Surround yourself with people who respect your boundaries
- True friends support your no
- Friends should never pressure you into anything unsafe
- Being a leader in safety inspires others to set boundaries too

Teach the mantra: "I protect myself, I protect my friends, and I protect my future."

Section 6: Self-Care After a Scary Moment

Sometimes, youth will feel anxious, embarrassed, or upset after standing up for themselves or reporting unsafe behavior.

Remind them:

- Their feelings are valid
- Talking to a trusted adult is healing
- Journaling or drawing can help process emotions
- Deep breaths and grounding exercises help regain control
- They are brave, strong, and responsible for keeping themselves safe

Self-care isn't selfish, it's self-preservation.

Section 7: Everyday Empowerment Practices

Youth can practice empowerment every day:

Repeat affirmations:

- "My body belongs to me."
- "No is my superpower."
- "I can protect myself."
- "I deserve respect."

Set micro-boundaries:

- Politely say no to unwanted hugs
- Decline invitations you're not comfortable with
- Speak up in small situations to build confidence

Reflect daily:

- Did I honor my boundaries today?
- Did I listen to my gut?
- Did I speak up when needed?

Practice leads to habits. Habits leads to lifelong empowerment.

Section 8: Real-Life Scenarios (Your Body, Your Rules)

Scenario 1: A peer insists on holding your phone

Action: "No, I want to hold it myself." Stand your ground.

Scenario 2: Someone wants a hug you don't want

Action: "No, thank you." Then you step back.

Scenario 3: A friend pressures you to share a secret about touching

Action: "I'm not sharing that. I will tell a safe adult."

Scenario 4: Online pressure to send photos or messages

Action: Stop communication. Block. Tell a trusted adult.

Scenario 5: Feeling unsafe somewhere alone

Action: Leave immediately. Find a safe adult or public space.

Youth should know: Every no is valid. Every boundary is valid. Every protective action is brave.

Section 9: Reflection Questions

1. What boundaries are most important to me?

2. How do I feel when I assert myself?

3. Who are my allies in keeping me safe?

4. What habits can I build to protect myself daily?

5. How can I encourage friends to respect their bodies too?

Chapter 10: Key Takeaways

• Your body belongs to you, always.

• Boundaries protect your safety, dignity, and confidence.

• Saying no is courageous, powerful, and enough.

• Confidence grows by practicing boundaries and speaking up.

• Surround yourself with people who respect you.

• Self-care is critical after scary or uncomfortable moments.

• Empowerment is a habit, practice it daily.

You made it to the end of section 1, and that says a lot about who you are. You're not just a kid flipping pages. You're becoming someone who leads with respect, protects others, and understands the weight of your own choices.

By now you know:

- **Respect starts with you**
- **"No" means stop**
- **Consent isn't optional**
- **Your body is yours**
- **And your hands were made to help, not harm**

These lessons aren't just rules. They're life-builders. Future-protectors. Character-shapers. The kind of truths that keep you from making mistakes you can't take back.

And here's the good news, when you choose respect, when you choose boundaries, when you choose kindness, you don't just keep yourself safe. You help build a world where everyone feels safe. That's how real change happens.

Not with fear. Not with shame. But with courage and truth, and kids like you choosing to be protectors, not hurters.

Carry these lessons with you. Teach them to your friends. Live them out loud. Your future is too bright to dim with choices that hurt others, or yourself.

Go forward with confidence and strength. You have the power to build the kind of world we all deserve, one respectful choice at a time. And remember, real love respects. Real leaders protect. And real success starts with doing what's right.

You have the power to protect your body, respect yourself, and set the rules for your life.

When youth understand:

• **Boundaries are non-negotiable**

• **Consent is mandatory**

• **Gut instincts are real**

• **Safe adults exist**

• **Digital safety matters**

• **Your body is yours, always**

…they grow into confident, empowered, and responsible adults who can protect themselves and others. Your body, your rules. Your voice, your power. Your safety, your responsibility, and your right.

PART 3

INTRO

When Rules Aren't Just Rules They're Protection

Before we step into this next part of your journey, let's get one thing clear: Your choices matter. Not just someday. Not just "when you're older." They matter now, today, in the hallways, the classrooms, the lunchrooms, and every place where you cross paths with someone else's body and boundaries.

This section isn't here to scare you. It's here to wake you up a little, the same way you'd tap a friend's shoulder to say, "Hey, pay attention. This part is important."

Because the truth is that grown folks don't always explain: Unwanted touching can turn your whole world upside down, fast. A joke, a dare, a moment of curiosity, or a split-second decision can lead to teachers stepping in, then principals, then police, and then judges. And suddenly, you're not the kid who made a mistake, you're the kid facing charges.

No child deserves to lose their freedom over something that could've been avoided with one simple habit: Respecting personal space and keeping your hands to yourself.

This section will show you:

- **How one touch can change everything,**
- **How quickly things get serious, and**
- **How to protect your future by making wise choices today.**

Think of this as your roadmap, the real-world version. No sugar-coating. No baby talk. Just the truth that keeps you safe, keeps you free, and keeps you on the path toward the successful life you're meant to have.

Now take a breath. Let's walk through the part that too many kids never get taught, until it's already too late.

When You Don't Keep Your Hands to Yourself

Chapter 1:

When a "Joke" Becomes a Crime

Why Touching Someone Without Permission Is Never Funny

Some kids think touching, grabbing, or poking someone is "just playing." They laugh. Their friends laugh. And for a moment, it looks like fun. But here's the truth no one tells you early enough: If everyone isn't laughing, it's not a joke, it's a problem.

When you touch someone without their permission, even as a joke, you cross a line that can change your life. That little moment can turn into something big:

- The person you touched feels scared, embarrassed, or disrespected.
- They tell a teacher, a coach, or a parent because they should.
- Adults step in, and suddenly it's not a joke anymore.

And here's the part kids don't know until it's too late: Unwanted touching has a name; assault. Even at your age, that's a serious word with serious consequences.

People get hurt. Friendships break. Trust disappears. Families get involved. And before you know it, someone has called the police.

One small moment can turn into:

- A write-up
- A suspension
- A police report
- Charges

And your life, your reputation, and your future take a turn you never expected. This chapter is here to warn you early: Keep your hands to yourself so you never have to learn this lesson the hard way.

When the Police Get Involved

Chapter 2:

The Real-Life Consequences That Come After a Bad Choice

Most kids have no idea how fast things can escalate once a report is made. But here's the real deal, when you touch someone without consent, adults don't have the option to just let it slide.

Once the police step in, here's what can happen:

1. Officers take statements from everyone. They listen to the person who was touched, to witnesses, and to you. They write everything down.

2. You may be taken to a juvenile office. Not always, but it happens. And sitting across from a police officer is not a fun or funny feeling.

3. You could face charges. Even as a kid. Even if you didn't mean it that way. Even if you were just playing.

Charges could include:

- **Simple assault**
- **Sexual assault**
- **Indecent contact**
- **Harassment**

These don't go away easily.

4. Your parents get called in.

And this is the moment everything shifts. The look on their faces. The fear in your heart. The disappointment everyone feels. The realization that everything changed over something that never needed to happen.

5. The other person's family is hurting too. They're worried. They're angry. They're heartbroken. Now you've got two families, two sets of friends (sometimes), and one moment that split everything. And again, it didn't have to happen. Let this chapter be your warning, your hands can write a story you never wanted to star in.

Courtrooms, Probation & Losing Your Freedom

Chapter 3:

**How One Choice
Can Follow You Into Your Future**

If charges move forward, things get even more serious. And too many kids don't realize how far this can go.

Here's what can happen when a case goes to court:

1. You stand before a judge. A real courtroom. Real rules. The judge listens to what happened and decides your consequences.

2. You may be placed on probation. Probation is not freedom.
It means:

- **Regular check-ins**
- **Behavior rules**
- **Curfews**
- **Counseling**
- **School reports**
- **Limited activities**

One more mistake can land you somewhere even more difficult.

3. You could be ordered to juvenile detention.

Jail for kids, but still jail. You lose:

- Your phone
- Your music
- Your friends
- Your room
- Your freedom

You go to bed when they say. You wake up when they say. You eat what they give you. You miss birthdays, games, vacations, and life.

4. Your record may follow you. Some charges stay sealed. Some don't. But one thing is guaranteed: You will never forget the experience.

And all of this because of a choice that could have been avoided with one simple rule: Keep Your Hands To Yourself. Touching someone without their permission isn't funny. It isn't small. It isn't harmless. It isn't a prank.

It's assault, and it can turn your whole world upside down. But here's the good news: You have the power to avoid all of this. You have the strength to make the right choices. You have the wisdom to walk away, ask questions, and respect boundaries. Your future is bright, protect it with your wise decisions!

OUTRO

The Power to Protect Your Future Is Already in Your Hands

Look at you, you just finished reading some tough truths. Not everyone your age gets this kind of knowledge. Some kids learn these lessons in a courtroom. Some learn them after someone gets hurt. Some learn them when they hear a judge say the words, "I'm placing you on probation."

But you? You're learning now, before any of that happens. And that's power. Real power. Here's what I want you to remember long after you close this book: You are responsible for your choices. And your choices shape your future.

Touching someone without consent, playing jokes that aren't funny, crossing boundaries because you didn't think it was that serious - those decisions can take away opportunities, friendships, freedom, and peace.

But respecting boundaries? That keeps doors open. That builds trust. That keeps your record clean and your future bright. That shows leadership, maturity, and self-control; the traits of someone going somewhere great in life.

Listen, there is nothing weak about walking away. There is nothing uncool about doing the right thing. And there is absolutely nothing funny about hurting someone else or risking your freedom.

Real strength is self-control. Real courage is respect. Real success begins with good choices.

So, as you move forward, carry this section with you, like a shield. Let it guide your hands. Let it guide your mind. Let it guide your heart.

Your life is valuable. Your future is waiting. Every moment and every decision is your chance to protect it. Now go on. Walk tall. Walk wise. And keep your hands to yourself! Your future will thank you for it.

ABOUT THE AUTHOR

Dr. Charmaine Marie is an educator, Best-Selling Author, and advocate committed to empowering youth through knowledge, boundaries, and self-respect. As an Amazon Best-Selling Author, she writes with purpose-creating age-appropriate, prevention-focused books that equip children with the language, confidence, and courage to protect themselves and respect others.

With a background in education and youth mentorship, Dr. Charmaine Marie is passionate about teaching life skills that are often overlooked but deeply necessary. Her work centers on helping young people understand personal boundaries, consent, healthy relationships, and the long-term impact of choices. She believes prevention begins with honest conversations, clear guidance, and adults who are willing to teach what matters before harm occurs.

Beyond writing, Dr. Charmaine Marie is a devoted mother, proud grandmother, community leader, and entrepreneur. She is the founder of Real LOVE Executive, a woman-owned luxury wine company, and she continues to serve families through education, advocacy, and leadership. Her mission is simple but powerful: to help raise informed, confident youth who grow into responsible, respectful, and successful adults.

We really appreciate you taking the time
to read, My Body My Rules
A Kid's Journey Into Boundaries & Bravery
Please do a review on Amazon.com
to let us know what you think.

www.ingramcontent.com/pod-product-compliance
Lightning Source LLC
Chambersburg PA
CBHW070510100426
42743CB00010B/1800